HEDGEHOG ART
THROUGH THE AGES

S. M. Bach and H.R.H. P. P. Pricklepants

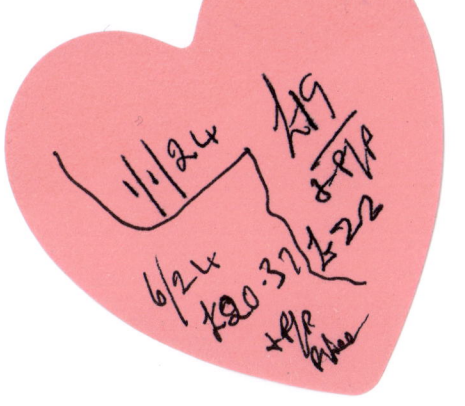

Copyright © 2016 S. M. Bach

All rights reserved.

ISBN:1539641880
ISBN-13: 978-1539641889

"Imagination is
the only weapon
in the war against
reality."

This book is dedicated to the best animal – hedgehogs.

CONTENTS

	Introduction	i
1	Renaissance Hedgehog Art	1
2	Baroque Hedgehog Art	9
3	Neoclassical Hedgehog Art	17
4	Hedgehog Romanticism	21
5	Modern Hedgehog Art	27
6	Hedgehog Americana	39
7	Japanese Hedgehog Art	47
8	Concluding Remarks	57

INTRODUCTION

Dear reader, we are delighted to present to you this collection of hedgehog art with critical commentary. The works in this book have been researched, analyzed, and sometimes even discovered by the authors, through many, many hours of work in Photoshop™. The field of hedgehog art history is surprisingly neglected in literature, blogs, Twitter, Facebook, and other sources for research, but has been increasingly significant in Hedgehog-American Studies. This field has popularized the Pricklepants Corollary: "any image can be somehow improved by adding a hedgehog." We hope this work helps to not only further confirm the Pricklepants Corollary, but also add valuable knowledge for the edification and betterment of all. Hedgehog art history is quite a young field with exciting discoveries still frequently made. In this brief volume we are excited to be able to share a some highlights from the more remarkable, interesting, and delightful works of hedgehog art. We sincerely hope you enjoy it.

1 RENAISSANCE HEDGEHOG ART

We commence our exploration of the wonderful world of hedgehog art in the Renaissance, a period when the fine arts were elevated above being a product of craftsmanship of artisans to works created by true artists who mastered many disciplines. So far as art goes, this art's uniquely well known for being so artistic, and is so influential that even today there are still Mutant Ninja Turtles named after the great artists of the period. The most talented artists of the era struggled to top one another's work in the Renaissance equivalent of rap battles, except with art, and taking a far longer time. The greats of this era expanded the creative fields, and developed new expressive ways of representing hedgehogs. In the following section we present a number of highlights.

We begin our journey with one of the most definitive works in Renaissance hedgehog art history. Michelangelo's original approach at painting the ceiling of the Sistine Chapel featured this powerful and truly stirring scene of the creation of hedgehogs. Sadly, the Vatican rejected Michelangelo's first design, this version only being saved by the work of several renegade Franciscans.

HEDGEHOG ART THROUGH HISTORY

While a less well known Botticelli work, his *Birth of a Hedgehog* is a beautiful and sublime early work of Florentine Renaissance hedgehog art in the "riccio" tradition. Like much in this tradition, it's rich in metaphor, calls back to Greco-Roman mythology, and features feet that look strange if you look at them for too long. Don't spend too much time looking at the feet.

So far as recent hedgehog art discoveries go, one of the most historic ties to the *Mona Lisa*. In early 2016, hedgehog art researchers at the Louvre applied laboratory spectral analysis using non-invasive laser analysis to the *Mona Lisa*. They made a truly remarkable discovery based on a recently discovered notebook by Leonardo Da Vinci. The notebook referred to the work as *La Gioconda con Riccio* (happiness with hedgehog), while underpainting analysis now confirms the original work is actually a masterwork of hedgehog art. These are exciting times for hedgehog art critics and historians. We now know what the original *Mona Lisa* looks like.

This second Da Vinci work, *Lady With a Hedgehog* (c.1488-1489) is a stunning example of Renaissance hedgehog art, masterfully executed. The human subject is not known with certainty, though the hedgehog is strongly believed by experts to be Contessa Mirandella di Pricklipanzia, a distant relation of Princess Perdita Pricklepants via the Venetian line of the family. While the hedgehog represented is an actual noble-hog, as a hedgehog she also serves as a symbol of elegance, grace, and impeccable manners.

We now reach Raphael, great artist of the High Renaissance, who along with Da Vinci and Michelangelo form the trinity of greats of the period. The enigmatic and sublime beauty of Raphael's early work, *Portrait of a Lady with a Hedgiecorn*, has been a subject hedgehog art critics have over-discussed for centuries. The influence of Da Vinci on Raphael's work is clearly seen here in the similarities to the *Mona Lisa* in pose, gaze, and format of this painting. Da Vinci's influence can also be seen in the use of a hedgehog, following Da Vinci's various Hedgehog Masterworks, and again symbolizing elegance, grace, and impeccable manners.

Donatello's first version of this statue created for the Vatican was titled, *St. Mark With Hedgehog* and was commissioned for St. Peter's Basilica. Sadly, Pope Leo X was not amused, and Donatello was forced to create another statue, this time without the hedgehog. One little known fact about this work is that Martin Luther was finally motivated to write his 95 theses because of Leo X's unwillingness to embrace hedgehog art (according to oral tradition).

This work marks a true high point in our excursion through hedgehog art, as we've now shown hedgehog artworks by Michelangelo, Leonardo, Raphael, and Donatello, which completes the Teenage Mutant Ninja Turtle sequence, and unlocks the next level – Baroque Hedgehog Art.

2 BAROQUE HEDGEHOG ART

The Baroque hedgehog art period is noted by greater contrasts of light and dark, especially in the quills and shadows of hedgehogs, along with hedgehogs sitting and standing more naturally. While our classifications are not the standard which limited anthropocentric art histories apply, these classifications are the norm for broader-scoped hedgehog art history. Hedgehog art critics are often warned to never use the "If it isn't Baroque, don't fix it" quip, due to risks of this being interpreted as either a critique of art preservation, or as a suggestion to only apply art conservation techniques to Baroque works. As a result we will refrain.

We begin with a Dutch Renaissance masterwork by Johannes Vermeer. Vermeer's work is notable not only for his skill of execution, but also for the significant number of forgeries. When *Hedgehog With a Pearl Earring* went to auction in 1947, it was widely considered by experts as a forgery of Vermeer done by the notorious Van Meegeren. Thanks to painstaking research by hedgehog art historians and conservationists, the provenance of this piece has been authoritatively recognized as a true Vermeer master-work.

Caravaggio's *Boy with a Basket of Fruit and Some Hedgehogs*, c. 1593, is a stunning work. The light, expressiveness, and technical execution are all superb. These elements illustrate the transition from the more constrained and austere styles of the Renaissance into the more dynamic, dramatic styles of the Baroque, as we can see by the pair of hedgehogs striking dramatic poses and the powerful lighting on the quills. Strangely, this work was not well accepted by the public. The culture of Renaissance Italy held unusual cultural superstitions regarding the idea of hedgehogs crawling in their food as "unclean." Caravaggio ultimately reworked the painting without hedgehogs (weakening the dynamics and drama the hedgehogs bring to the work). The hedgehog edition was forgotten until 2014 when it was rediscovered by a shopper who bought the painting at a Goodwill in West Covina, California.

While traditionalist anthropocentric art historians would be writing this section about Rembrandt's *Belshazzar's Feast With Hedgehog*, we just need to add that Caravaggio's dynamic work with light and shadow had a huge influence on Baroque art, as can be seen here. This painting was an enigma to hedgehog art historians for decades until it was discovered that Rembrandt had initially read a faulty Dutch translation of the book of Daniel that had translated the word "Writing" as "Hedgehog." This work is housed in the National Hedgehog Gallery, London.

HEDGEHOG ART THROUGH HISTORY

Hidden for centuries, Rembrandt's 1661 *Portrait of a Lady With a Hedgehog* is a high point in Baroque Hedgehog Art. While not as well known as his *Belshazzar's Feast With Hedgehog*, this late work of Rembrandt's highlights his masterful use of light, composition, and hedgehogs. The work was only discovered post-WW II, having been lost in the basement of the Rijksmuseum.

A hedgehog art historian's rewards are mostly small pleasures, so we take small pleasure in announcing a small first in that we bring a third example of an artist's works. Rembrandt, being one of the all time great painters and great artists. If we had to use only one word to describe Rembrandt's 1652 *Aristotle with a Hedgehog* it would be "painting," which is why we tend to use more words.

HEDGEHOG ART THROUGH HISTORY

Rembrandt's, Portrait of Hedgehog Noble (1653) is another first by being the first time there's a fourth painting by the same artist, but we will not let that distract from this magnificent work. If some pictures are worth a thousand words, this one is worth far more. There are so many things that could be said about this incredible tour de force, literal mountains of books could be penned, and still more would remain waiting to be said, hence this is a favorite work for hedgehog art critics to write about, debate, and generally discuss. The obvious discussability of this work and all its implications are so self-evident that we leave it to the reader to compose their own 1000 word essay. Please self-grade by word count.

3 NEOCLASSICAL HEDGEHOG ART

Neoclassical hedgehog art is classical hedgehog art, but starting with the prefix, "neo." Modeled on Greco-Roman aesthetic ideals, and often depicting allegorical scenes from Classical mythology, but exploring the various new paint colors, sophisticated techniques to achieve a naturalistic realism, and other artistic advancements, these works are beautiful, striking, and tend to feature hedgehogs in quite dramatic composition.

Here we present a work by Jacques-Louis David, iconic painter through the French Revolution and Napoleons's reign. His 1786 *The Discomfort of Socrates* details the event of the initial cup of hedgehog handed to Socrates, because the jailer misheard "hemlock." David's masterful rendering of the cup being handed over is a truly powerfully captured expression of awkwardness. Created by David for Napoleon's palace, the painting was poorly received, and has been much less popular than the later version.

Alma-Tadema's 1884 "A Reading from Homer to a Hedgehog" is a lovely late Victorian painting. Through attention to details such as architecture and dress, Alma-Tadema's work beautifully and imaginatively re-created everyday life for hedgehogs in ancient times. Notice the attentive expression of the hedgehog, paying rapt attention to the poem's recitation.

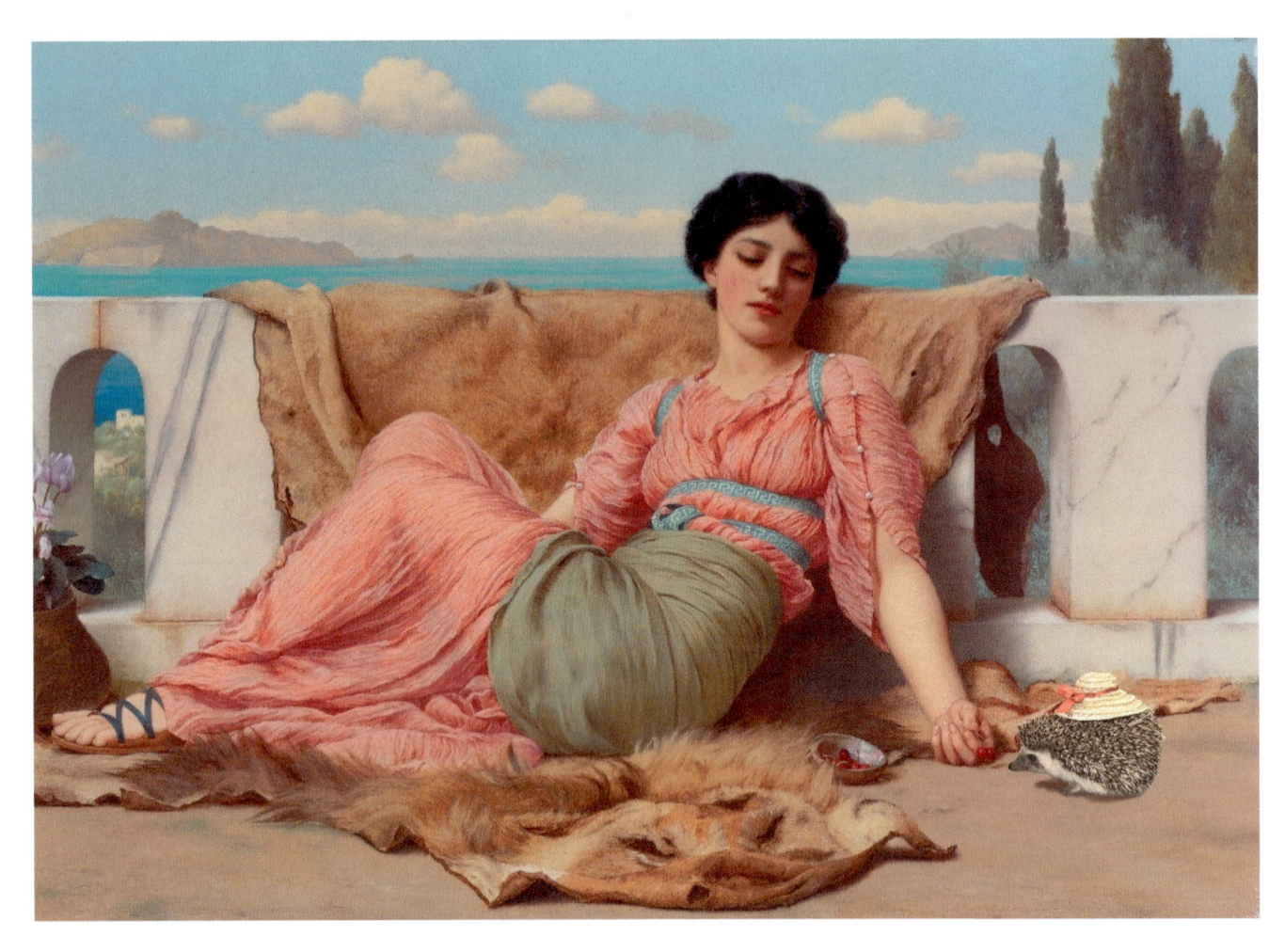

John William Godward's 1905 *A Quiet Pet Hedgehog* is a lovely, if confused example of neoclassical hedgehog art. The hand in this image is feeding the hedgehog cherries, which makes no sense – hedgehogs do not like cherries. There are two schools of thought as to what this fact means. The first group of critics believe Godward was simply shockingly unfamiliar with what sort of things a hedgehog would like to eat. The second group are allegorists who believe the hedgehog, hat, cherries, lion skin, etc. each are part of a complex story, though each critic has their own unique interpretation of the symbolism. Some have said that this is evidence that hedgehog art critics clearly have too much time on their hands, though the reality is much more complex and nuanced than that.

4 HEDGEHOG ROMANTICISM

Romanticism arrived as a reaction to the intellectualizing and seriousness of the Classical hedgehog art tradition. Instead artists focused on depth of emotion and more dramatic material, capturing the breadth and scale of the inner life and experience of hedgehogs. Here we present a collection of dramatic and emotionally powerful highlights.

Once discovered, Caspar David Friedrich's *Wanderer Above the Sea of Hog* (c. 1817) quickly became an iconic hedgehog work from the Romantic period. The self-reflective pose and invitation to see things from the hedgehog's perspective make this an incredibly powerful work which has been featured on the covers of hedgehog books, hedgehog album covers, and has become part of modern hedgehog culture.

Johann Peter Krafft's 1855 *Faust on Easter Morning Holding a Hedgehog* was based on a confusion due to the similarities between the German word for hedgehog, "Egel," and the German word for selling one's soul to gain knowledge, "faustischen Pakt." It was corrected in a subsequent version. Despite being a mistake, this version holds a special place in the hearts of hedgehog art historians since it was an understandable mistake, and because it's a painting that has a hedgehog in it.

This portrait of Sir Brooke Boothby (by Joseph Wright) is a notable though less well known work of hedgehog art. In the words of noted hedgehog art critic, Paris Quillton, this work displays "sweet, sweet style." Note the symbolic posing in nature with a copy of Rousseau's essays and the symbolic hedgehog.

Jan Van Beers' 1884 *The Letter and the Hedgehog* is lovely in evoking the sense of a hedgehog and lady in conversation:
"Isn't it lovely to sit on the edge of a cliff peering wistfully at things?"
"Oh, indeed, it's so lovely to look down at the rocky shore several thousand feet below, isn't it?"
(Contented Sigh)
(Contented Sigh)

John Singer Sargent's *Portrait of Madame X With Hedgehog* (1884) was an incredibly scandalous painting when it was revealed in a salon to Parisian society. At the time, hedgehogs were not well accepted in portraiture and controversy ensued. Sargent eventually painted over the hedgehog, though, alas the painting was still scandalous, since one the hedgehog was removed, the sensuous portrait of Virginie Amélie Avegno Gautreau was noticed and people were up in arms again. Sargent's troubles in Paris spelled success in the US and UK, so in the end things worked out for him. The original under-painting seen here was recently discovered via advances in spectroscopy and sophisticated imaging technologies. Hopefully you won't be scandalized.

5 MODERN HEDGEHOG ART

Modern hedgehog art is known for freedom of form (and sometimes freedom from form) and its pointed subversiveness, and general weirdness which is why it's a favorite domain for every hedgehog art historian.

Van Gogh's 1888 *The Starry Hedgehog Night* was a view painted from the east-facing window of his asylum room. The nurses notices the various hedgehogs hidden in the painting and were concerned, so Vincent repainted the more well known version of the painting. Much could be said, though it's better to just look at it.

HEDGEHOG ART THROUGH HISTORY

Here we present a second historic work by Vincent van Gogh, *Irises and Also a Hedgehog*. An immediately striking painting created in the last year before his death in 1890, he considered this painting the study on which the later more famous hedgehog-lacking Iris painting was based on, though it stands alone as a sublime and magnificent work of post-Impressionist hedgehog art.

The Persistence of Hedgehog by Salvador Dali (1930) is both weird and a milestone in surrealist hedgehog art. It's currently displayed in the Museum of Modern Hedgehog Art in New York.

Continuing with surrealism, René Magritte's *Le Fils de l'Herrison* is very complicated to explain, but here it is.

Ceci n'est pas une hérisson.

Magritte

This surrealist work, Magritte's *The Treachery of Hedgehog Images* (1928), was not well understood by critics he initially showed the work to. Rather than taking an interest in the distinction between the symbol and what is symbolized, they exclaimed things like, "oh, a hedgehog, they're the best" (in French) which irritated the easily annoyed Magritte. He later approached the painting a second time using a pipe which became somewhat famous. The original is currently held in a private collection.

Alphonse Mucha's *P. Pricklepants* is a masterful Art Nouveau work from 1898. This work appears to have been a commission by the Grand Marchioness Pricklepants of Paris. The work simply exudes loveliness, which illustrates why Hedgehog art historians often find this period visually risky, as many who venture here grow hyper-focused.

Her Highness has been somewhat focused on Mucha's work, so here is Alphonse Mucha's, *Hedgehog Princess Perusing Art*, c. 1890. This is a truly lovely later work by Mucha, who clearly had a fondness for hedgehogs. Unfortunately, little is known about this work, though the greater subtlety and simpler composition than *P. Pricklepants* suggest this work was inspired by different themes.

Hérisson

Little is known about Alphonse Mucha's *Perdita* (1918). While it's believed to have been created by Mucha in Paris in 1918, the work is something of a mystery to hedgehog art historians, as the identity of the hedgehog is unknown, and the origin/purpose of the work is not documented. In this case, the air of mystery adds an evocative layer of wonder to an already wonderful piece.

Maxfield Parrish's 1921 *Hedgehog Break* is regarded as one of the most popular hedgehog art prints of the 20th century. Parrish later produced the human-centric *Daybreak*, which went on to even greater fame, though he always considered this work's composition and symbolism as more powerful.

Jackson Pollock's 1951 *The Convergence of Quills* was produced by splattering paint on a canvas incredibly cleverly so the result looked like a hedgehog. His agent suggested instead of a hedgehog he just make a similar version that was just mess of splatters that different people would see all kinds of things in, with the result that this earlier version was all but forgotten for decades.

Four Hedgehogs (1962). This work was accidentally left in the basement of the Tate and only discovered in 2016. Initially critics assumed the work to be some kind of parody of Warhol, while now art critics debate whether it's parody, self-parody, meta-ironic parodying of self-parody, or one of the other kinds of things art critics argue about. As with much in modern art, it's very hard to explain.

HEDGEHOG ART THROUGH HISTORY

6 HEDGEHOG AMERICANA

In the United States, African pygmy hedgehogs, like most Americans, are descended from immigrants to the US. Due to this and numerous other things, they are in their way the most American animal. While there is no saying that goes, "There's nothing more American than hedgehogs, baseball, and/or apple pie," because it's not as catchy as it could be, The Hedgehog–American Cultural Association is working on a better slogan which points to an important insight – hedgehogs: they are very American. In this section we present a collection of iconic American hedgehog art.

We begin our excursion into Americana with the most American hedgehog art within the bounds of human conceivability: Emanuel Leutze's *Hedgehog Crossing the Delaware*, a true high point of 1850s America's hedgehog art — noble but realistic sniffing poses, stirring imagery, truly remarkable artistic composition.

James Whistler's 1870 *Whistler's Hedgie Mom* is a landmark work. He eventually convinced his mother to pose without her pets. It is exhibited in and held by the Musée d'Hérissons in Paris.

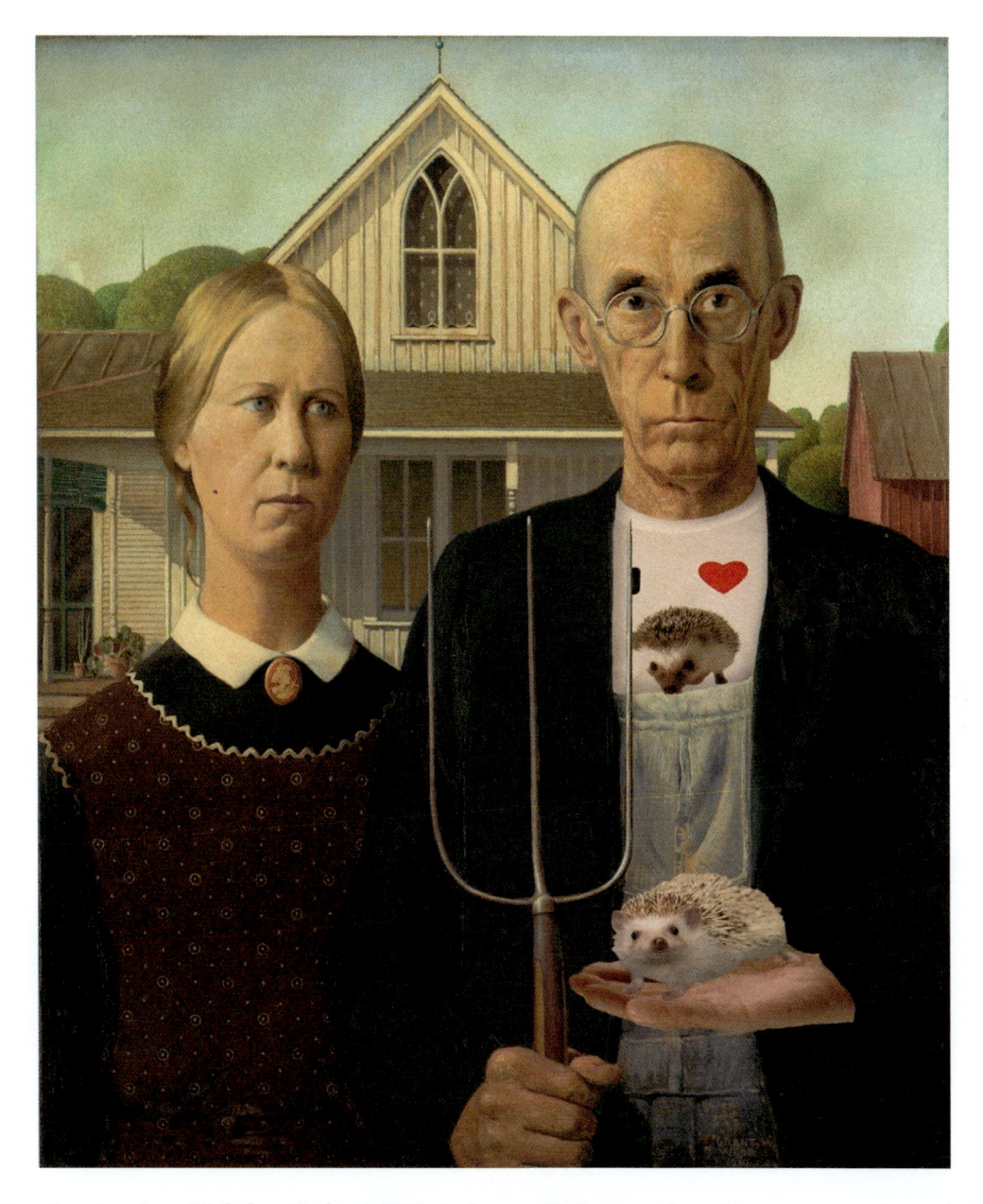

Grant Wood's *American Hedgehog Gothic* (1928) is less well known than his more popular painting, but this remarkable piece is truly iconic in American hedgehog art and culture.

Edward Hopper's *Nighthogs* was recently discovered in museum archives of the Art Institute of Chicago among works willed by Hopper to the museum that were long neglected in storage vaults. It's very exciting to see this remarkable discovery come to light.

Hogs Playing Poker by Cassius Marcellus Coolidge (yes, that really is his name) has generally been looked down upon by art critics who accuse the work of being faddish, kitschy, lowbrow culture, and a poor-taste parody of "genuine" art, which is why modern art critics are not worth listening to. Several critics who aren't jerks have noted that this work was very significant in helping bring hedgehog art into the modern mainstream in America, and point out Coolidge careful studied and used motifs, styles, and composition from Caravaggio, Cezanne, and other greats of hedgehog art.

Norman Rockwell's love of hedgehogs is not widely known, which is truly unfortunate. Rockwell made this painting as a cover for the Saturday Evening Post in 1958. At the time, featuring an African pygmy hedgehog on the cover in the diner was a brave move by Mr. Rockwell, but unfortunately the theme was too controversial and was ultimately not accepted until it was reworked.

HEDGEHOG ART THROUGH HISTORY

7 JAPANESE HEDGEHOG ART

The artistic traditions of Japan were unique both in aesthetic principles, and in how frequently the hedgehog was featured as a subject, especially in their ukiyo-e woodblock print making tradition. These works are so lovely and sometimes so subtle we'll keep commentary to a minimum to avoid distraction.

Utagawa Kunimasa's 1803 *Woman with Hedgehog*.

Katsushika Hokusai *Hedgehog Views Mount Fuji* (1828)

Katsushika Hokusai *Courtesan Asleep, and also a Hedghog* (1800)

Katsushika Hokusai *Hedgehog Riding the Great Wave* (c. 1835?). There's some debate about the authenticity of this work.

HEDGEHOG ART THROUGH HISTORY

Hokusai's Hedgehog on *The Suspension Bridge on the Border of Hida and Etchū Provinces* (c. 1830), part of his series, "Remarkable Views of Bridges in Various Provinces with Hedgehogs On Them."

Another hedgehog art history milestone: Utagawa Hiroshige's 1852, *Tubing after Snow at Kameyama*.

Taiso Yoshitoshi's *Hedgehog Princess Peering at Moon from Cliff* (1885) is most notable for being notable. If you look carefully at this image, you may spot several ninjas, though they are very good at hiding, so you probably won't.

Toshi Yoshida's *Hedgehog Parachuting amid Cherry Blossoms* (1953) is a very remarkable print, not only for its subject and composition, but for the daring and clever symbolism of the work, which while difficult to translate, is something you'd think was really, really cool if you knew what it was about.

Kunisada's *Dawn at Futami-ga-ura with Hedgezilla*, c. 1962 was a very late era ukiyo-e print. The subject matter was unusual for Kunisada, and for ukiyo-e artists in general. Hedgezilla would go on to make a number of successful films.

Kobayashi Kiyochika's 1958 *Mecha-Hedgezilla Preparing to Attack Shin Ohashi Bridge* is fascinating both as a later masterful example of ukiyo-e print making, and a noteworthy early representation of Mecha-Hedgezilla.

8 CONCLUDING REMARKS

We hope you've enjoyed this journey through hedgehog art of the ages. We've only offered a limited selection of various fascinating and wonderful hedgehog-related works in a field that continues to grow. If you would like to find more hedgehog art, the adventures of Princess Pricklepants, information about Hedgezilla, Hedgehog superheroes such as Bat-Hog, among other delightful things, please visit us at:

https://princesspricklepants.com

If you follow us on social media (Facebook/Twitter) in addition to finding irrefutable evidence of the Pricklepants Corollary ("any image can be somehow improved by adding a hedgehog"), you'll also find regular posts sharing delights and wonders in hedgehog arts and entertainment.

Our marketing team tells us we must mention that if one visits:

http://urchinwear.net

one will find a delightful and remarkable selection of tee shirts, some featuring artworks from this book, which if worn, may cause the wearer to be seen as cool by all the people they'd most want to be seen as cool by, and prove to the world they have amazingly discriminating taste. For non-US residents, notecards, etc. there are options here:

https://princesspricklepants.com/delightful-merch/

(Note: while we all wish otherwise, these works are not actual works, but parodies of great works of art. Surprising, indeed, but true.)

ABOUT THE AUTHORS

Princess Perdita Pricklepants, Grand Duchess of Tiggy-Winkle, Defender of Hufflepuff, Empress of Quillonia, and Dominions beyond the Seas is one of the foremost experts in hedgehog art, literature, and cinema, as well as a Startup Founder extraordinaire, Presidential Candidate, Etiquette Expert, Blogger of Wonder, Pirate Adventurer, Space Explorer, and Practically Perfect Hedgehog, among many other things.

S.M. Bach is ever her faithful handservant.

Printed in Great Britain
by Amazon